The Nit kit

To be a Natural Investigator, you need a **Nit kit**. Collect as many of these things together as you can:

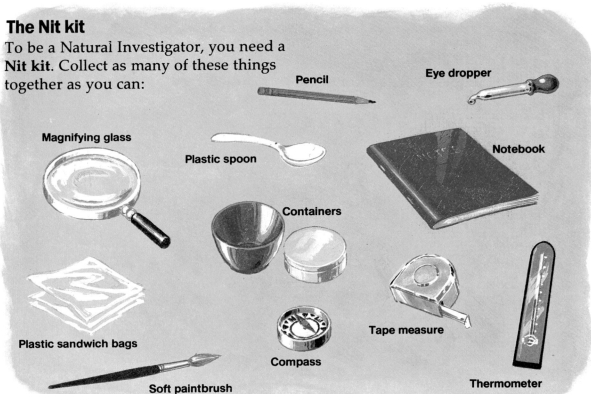

Pencil

Eye dropper

Magnifying glass

Plastic spoon

Notebook

Containers

Plastic sandwich bags

Compass

Tape measure

Thermometer

Soft paintbrush

Some investigations need other, special equipment which you can make or collect. You will find them as you go through the book.

There are plenty of ideas in this book for tests and experiments.

So where do you start? Follow the footsteps.

Habitats are everywhere!
In your garden, in the park, or anywhere you are safe.

This picture shows the habitats you will explore with this book. A habitat is a place that is just right for the animals and plants which live in it.

LOOKING AT NATURE

Written by
Robin Robbins

Illustrated by
Steve Holden, Keith Howard,
Glenn Steward and Michael Strand.

Designed by
Anthony Bussey

Edited by
Cathy Gaulter

The idea for the book comes from the BBC School Radio programme SCIENCE NATURALLY *(formerly* LOOKING AT NATURE*) presented by Timmy Mallett and Robin Robbins. It owes much to the help, support and good ideas of the programme's producer, Mike Howarth.*

About this book

Are you a Natural Investigator?

If you are reading this book, you are sure to be interested in the animals and plants you see around you. But a true Natural Investigator does not read everything from a book. Real members of the Natural Investigators' Team (the NITS for short!) find things out for themselves, like this:

Look! This beetle has just been found under a log. Beetles always have hard wing cases, with a line right down the middle.

Make a test! Does the beetle always choose to be in a dark place?

Dark part

Light part

Clear lid

Box

Challenge your test Do other beetles always live under things in the dark? Remember to let the beetles go free.

Is it always true? Does every kind of beetle live in the same sort of place? Finding things out is fun, and it makes you feel good too.

The wall

The north side

Wall watching is much more fun than you think, and the older and more crumbly the wall, the better the hunting for plants and animals. Best of all, use a compass to choose a wall that has a north and a south side, and compare the wildlife on each side.

Wet wall test Life on a dry wall is tough for plants because they need water as well as sunlight. On a damp day after rain, find out which part of the wall stays wettest for the plants. Stick a square of paper kitchen towel high up on the wall, and one very low down. Which one gets damp first? Are there more plants growing where the paper was wettest?

Squash a few leaves inside a sheet of kitchen towel.

See the wet green mark left by the water store.

Unfolding ferns

Ferns grow in the dampest places on the wall. The fronds start curled up like a spring. Watch one unfold!

Moss maps

Tiny green moss plants can grow in the smallest patch of damp dust. See if you can find the kinds in the picture. Do any of them grow on the driest part of your wall? Draw a moss map to show where each kind grows.

Water bottle leaves

Stonecrop can grow in dry places because it stores water inside its tiny thick leaves. Try this.

Pick a piece of stonecrop.

Make drawings of the frond as it unfolds and grows.

Late in summer, look underneath for the special pattern of brown marks called 'sori'. Ferns do not have flowers, but they spread a fine dust from their sori to make new ferns. Each speck of this dust is called a spore.

The north side

Ivy

Wall pennywort

Wren

Hart's tongue fern

Polypody fern

Banded snail

The south side

Wall screw moss

Funnel spider web

Lichen

Lichen

Zebra spider

Stonecrop

The south side

The south side of the wall gets hot and dry on sunny summer days. Few plants grow here, except for crusty lichens which can survive for a long time without rain.

Hot spots   Measure the temperature at the top and bottom of the wall. Mark the warmest spots with chalk.

Sunbathers on the wall   These creatures are *invertebrates*—animals without backbones. They must warm up before they can move quickly so they rest on the sunny wall in the morning. Do they choose your chalked warm spots for their sunbathing?

Bluebottle   Grasshopper   Greenbottle   Hoverfly

Hunters on the prowl   Other invertebrates will eat the sunbathers. This zebra spider is hunting for prey on the warm wall.

But the *segestria* spider builds a funnel web and traps its food.

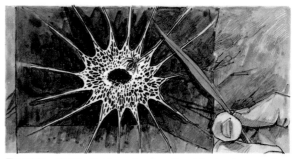

Try this   Tickle the funnel web with a blade of grass. If you tremble it as if you were a struggling fly, out will bounce the spider to catch it!

Detective work   In winter, most spiders die. So then you can pull the web out of the wall with a crochet hook. You will find skins of creatures the spider caught. What kinds are they?   Look carefully, and you will find spider skins of different sizes. As the spider grows, it splits each tight skin. A new, bigger one is ready underneath.

Build a home!
Use old bricks or stones to build a wall if there is no wall in your garden. It need not be very big. The wildlife will soon find it!

Bushes and hedges

Look out for the wonderful creatures which live in the bush habitat. Start with a spider safari!

Spider diamonds

Use a plant spray to spangle a web with water. Do the water drops stick to every part of it? Some threads are sticky. Gently touch the web with a paintbrush to find which ones. Watch where the spider puts her feet!

Make a 'lookerunderer' The spider hides under a leaf keeping one foot on a thread of the web. Then it can feel the tremble as the trapped insect struggles.

Make a lookerunderer like the one in the picture to find spiders hiding and waiting under leaves near their webs.

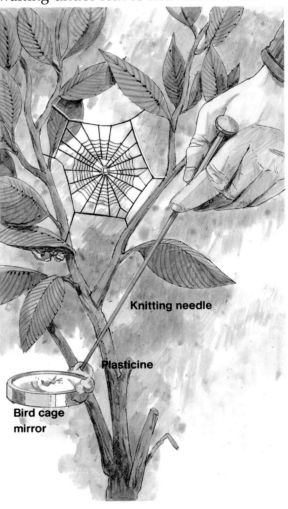

Knitting needle

Plasticine

Bird cage
mirror

Food parcels Some spiders use the sticky threads in their webs to trap insects for food. If you are lucky, you might see the spider roll its victim in a parcel of silk. Sometimes you can tell what kind of creature is wrapped inside.

Spot the difference
Each sort of spider makes its own special web. Can you find the differences between these webs?

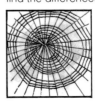 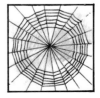

Hammock webs This web looks like a hammock hung up on the bushes. Test the web with the paintbrush to see if it is sticky. Can you guess how the web works? Look for the spider hanging upside-down underneath waiting for lunch to drop in!

Hunters on the run The wolf spider hunts its prey on the ground without using a web. In summer, watch out for the female carrying a bundle of eggs under her body.

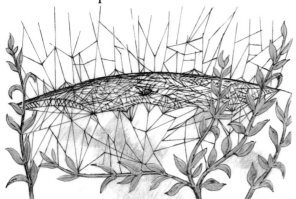

The bottom of the bushes

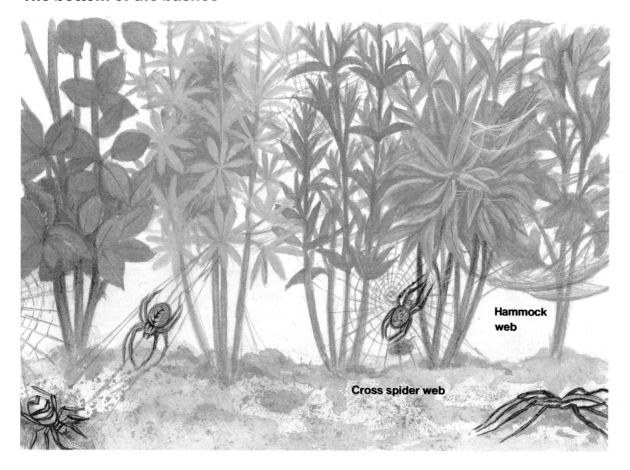

Hammock web

Cross spider web

Who else lives in the bush?

Other creatures use bushes as their habitat, and you will need sharp eyes to find them. They have many ways of keeping safe from their enemies.

Search for signs Damaged leaves

The leaf-cutter bee returns to the same plant to cut pieces from the leaves. She carries them away under her body. Wait until she comes back then follow her and see where she is using the leaves to make her nest.

A caterpillar holds the leaf with its feet and nibbles away at the edges. If you find a leaf like this, hunt close by for the caterpillar.

The small magpie moth rolls a leaf round itself and fastens it with silk. Inside its leaf larder it can munch away in safety hidden from the birds.

The leaf miner is a tiny caterpillar which burrows for safety right inside a leaf, making a tunnel as it munches. The tunnel gets wider as the caterpillar grows!

The top of the bushes

Ladybird

Ladybird larva

Leaf-cutter bee

Leaf mine

Privet hawkmoth caterpillar

Who eats who?

All living things depend on each other for food. So who eats who in the rose bush? Which creatures depend on the greenfly and the sweet sticky honeydew it makes on the leaves?

Rose bush food web   The bluetit might be caught by a cat or a kestrel, but the ladybird is safe because it tastes so nasty.

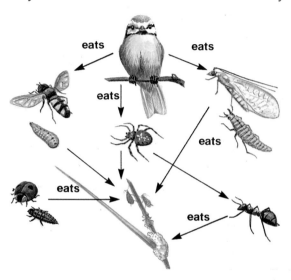

Caterpillar farm   If you want to watch a caterpillar grow, collect it gently with the soft paintbrush from your **Nit kit**. Pick a piece of the plant it was eating, and set up a caterpillar farm like this.

Growing up   Never let a caterpillar go without its own special food plant. A caterpillar's skin does not stretch like ours. It splits the old, tight one and there will be a new, bigger one underneath. The last time this happens the caterpillar changes into a **pupa**. This

means that it rests inside a special skin and changes into a butterfly or moth. Do not be surprised if your caterpillar burrows into the damp soil to pupate. Keep it in a cool place and remember to check it every week.

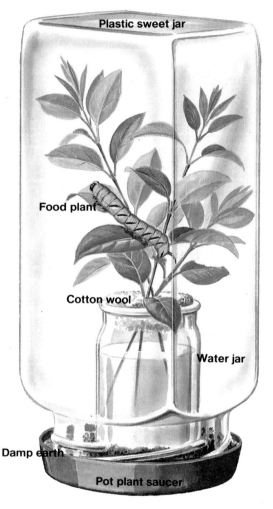

Bird garden

Birds in summer

Make your garden interesting for birds, with good food, nesting places and water for drinking and bathing. Then it will be interesting for you too!

Warning! If there are birds nesting in your garden, do not go near! Frightened birds may fly away and leave their babies to die.

Nesting materials

Mix wet mud with grass and put it in a tray outside. Which birds collect it for their nests?

Collect different things you think would be useful for nest making. Hang them up in a tree and see if the birds agree with you! Which material goes first?

Some birds will chase away other birds that come too close to their nests. Watch the male blackbirds fighting over their territories. Do they ever really hurt each other?

Feather care Birds will enjoy the water you put out for washing, and they will also like a dry, sandy spot for dust bathing.

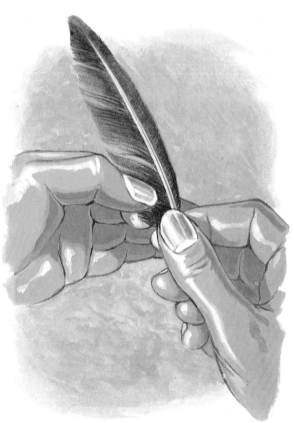

Birds use their beaks to pull their feathers into good shape. This is called **preening**. Pull a gap in the side of a feather. Then make your fingers into a beak and preen the feather whole again.

Late in summer the birds start to moult. This is a good time to start a feather collection.

The bird garden in summer

Fluff

Hay

String

Wool

Dust bath

Wet mud and hay

The bird garden in winter

Paper
hide

Cotoneaster

Dustbin lid

Bricks

Night-
light

Watching birds in winter

In winter, extra birds will come to your bird garden. Even the shyer ones will move in during hard weather if you give them food.

A window hide   Use sticky tape to fasten big sheets of paper over your window. Make eye holes at just the right height so you can watch the birds without disturbing them. The birds often come very close!

Favourite foods   Which are the best-sellers in your bird take-away restaurant? Make a fair test to find out. Collect several small dishes, all exactly the same. Choose some different foods, and put one kind of food in each dish and level it off at the top. Put the dishes outside and use your window hide to see which food is eaten first.

A bird bubble   Some bully birds frighten the smaller kinds away and eat more than their share of food. Solve this by making a 'bird bubble'.

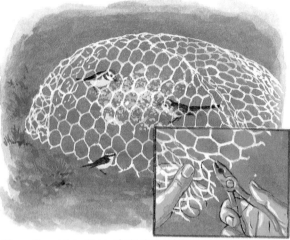

You will need a piece of chicken wire roughly a metre square, and with holes of about 5 centimetres across. Use pliers to bend it into a bubble shape. Then you can put some food out under the bubble. The smaller species can easily go inside, but the bigger ones cannot!

Bird berries   If you can, plant some berry bushes to give the birds winter food. Choose from their favourites, such as firethorn, cotoneaster, hawthorn and holly. Plant them close to the window hide so you can watch the birds feeding.

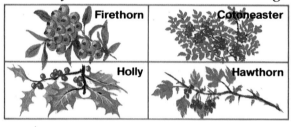

They need a drink too!   In very cold weather, drinking water is just as important as food. One way of keeping the water free from ice is to put a nightlight under a metal dish of water. A dustbin lid makes a good dish, but not if it is plastic! Ask for help before you light the candle.

Grass

Life in the lawn

Short grass is not a good habitat for many creatures. There is nowhere to hide, and not much to eat. But underneath, hundreds of worms are busy!

Try worm charming! Choose a dewy morning and tread up and down on the spot. Different kinds of worms will wriggle out of the ground near your feet. Use your **Nit kit** magnifying glass to spot the differences between them.

Worm work Some worms pull leaves into their burrows for food. Look for a worm hole with a rolled leaf stuck in it. Put a circle of different kinds of leaves round a worm hole. Draw them in your notebook and come back next day. Which kind of leaf did your worm choose? Is it always the same every time?

Short grass plants
Plants like daisies and clover grow their leaves very close to the ground. The lawnmower does not harm them when it cuts the grass.

Lazy daisy Hundreds of years ago, the daisy was called a 'day's eye'. To find out why, put a flower pot over a daisy flower for an hour or so. What happens to it when it gets dark?

Worm watch Ask if you may watch the worm hole at night. Worms are not frightened by red light, so use a torch covered with thin red plastic. You might see the worm pulling a leaf into its burrow. Tread very softly, or it will quickly go back down the hole.

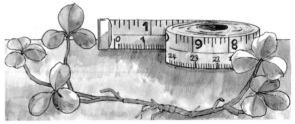

The clover trail Find some white clover in the grass and give it a little tug. You will see it is joined to other clover plants in a string called a **runner**. Use a tape measure to find the longest chain of plants in the grass.

Short grass plants

Dandelion

Starlings

Daisy

Clover

Flocking for food   The starlings poke across the short grass looking for worms, slugs, and leatherjackets to eat. A leatherjacket is a cranefly larva. The larva changes into a pupa, and later on, into an adult flying insect.

The cranefly

Larva

Pupa

Adult

Make a trap!   You can catch craneflies and other insects as they change from pupae to adults ready to fly away.

To make your trap, you will need two wire coat hangers, an empty jam jar, some thin fabric, and a pair of wire cutters.

To make your trap cut the wire at the bottom of the hangers and open them out.

Fasten them together at the top with string or sticky tape and cross them over each other.

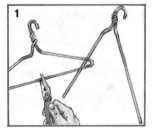

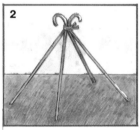

Cut your fabric to the right shape—measure first! Glue or sew it over the coat hanger frame like a tent. Leave a gap at the top, with the extra fabric hanging down.

Stick the trap into the ground, and put the jar over the top with the loose material tucked in. Leave it outside for a day and a night! Look in the jar for your catch.

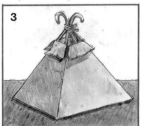

The long grass habitat

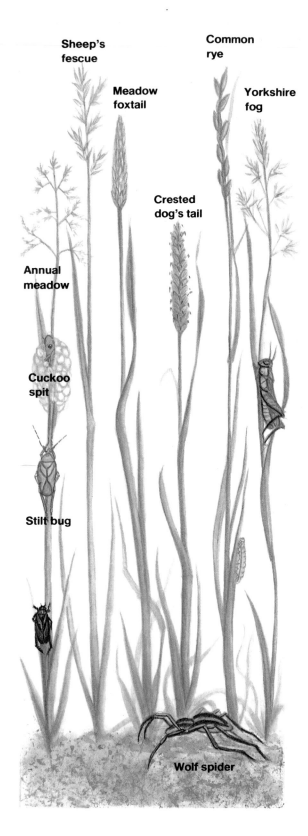

Sheep's fescue

Common rye

Meadow foxtail

Yorkshire fog

Crested dog's tail

Annual meadow

Cuckoo spit

Stilt bug

Wolf spider

Grow some grasses

You can usually find a patch of long grass in a park, but to investigate grass flowers at home, leave just a corner of the lawn unmown right through the spring until June or July.

Grass flowers Grasses have beautiful flowers with rich colours. At first they look like green tufts among the grass blades, but use your magnifying glass and be ready for a surprise! Collect just one stem of each kind to help you to make some really huge paintings!

Flowers and seeds

Give a sharp flick to a flowering grass head, and watch a cloud of pollen puff out. The grass cannot make seeds unless some pollen touches the feathery part of the flower, called the **stigma**. The pollen blows in the wind from one grass to another. Can you see which part of the grass flower makes the pollen? It is called the **anther**.

Stigma

Anther

Knowing the names Some grasses have wonderful names which give clues to the kinds you have found. A crested dog's tail looks just like one, and so does a meadow foxtail! But why do you think the soft, greeny-pink kind is called Yorkshire fog?

Long grass habitat
Many small creatures live in the long grass, munching away at the leaves and stems. You need a net to catch some!

Make a sweep net Find a wire coat hanger, a plastic carrier bag, and some sticky tape. A clear plastic carrier is best if you can get one.

Bend the coat hanger into a diamond shape.

Put one handle of the carrier bag over the coat hanger hook, and tuck the bag opening over the wire diamond shape you made. Use the sticky tape to fasten the bag top firmly in place.

Swish the bag to and fro through the long grass. After a few swishes, turn the net upside-down, so no creatures can escape.

To move the creatures into your collecting jars, you will need to put both hands inside the net, holding the jar in one hand and its lid in the other. It takes quite a lot of practice!

Camouflage Although most grassland animals are green, some are patterned with other colours. Make some cut-out pictures of one of your creatures. Colour each one differently and put it in the grass. Which colour makes the best camouflage?

Don't just trap! Set all your creatures free again. You can come back later to find out about the secret lives in the grassland jungle.

Flower beds

Garden flowers come in all shapes and sizes, but you will always be able to find anthers and stigmas! Most of them use insects rather than the wind to carry pollen from one flower to another. You can see the pollen grains caught up in the insects' fur.

Favourite flower colour

Make a chart like this and count the number of insect visitors to each colour. Another choice chart could show if both bees and flies choose the same colours.

Bumble bee burglars

Look for flower shapes which make it hard for burglars! For example, only heavy insects, like bumble bees, can press open the mouth of the snapdragon and get inside.

Use your finger to push on the snapdragon's bottom lip. How hard does a bee have to press? Find the anthers and decide which part of the bee's fur will catch the pollen to carry it away to another snapdragon.

Do bees remember?

Choose a sunny spot, and leave a bunch of flowers there, in the bees' favourite colour. Watch the bees visiting the flowers. After an hour of 'buzziness', take the flowers away, but keep watching. Do the bees come back to look for them?

Flower magic

As the sun goes down, watch the flower bed to see how the flowers get ready for night. Some close up, some turn their heads down, and some stay open waiting for night-flying insects to visit them.

But one magic flower, the evening primrose, saves its pollen and nectar for the night-time moths. Stand and listen and you will hear its petals rustle as you watch the flowers unfold. Its strong perfume calls the moths to visit it.

Flower bed habitat

Sunflower

Policeman's helmet

Pansy

Snapdragon

How seeds leave home

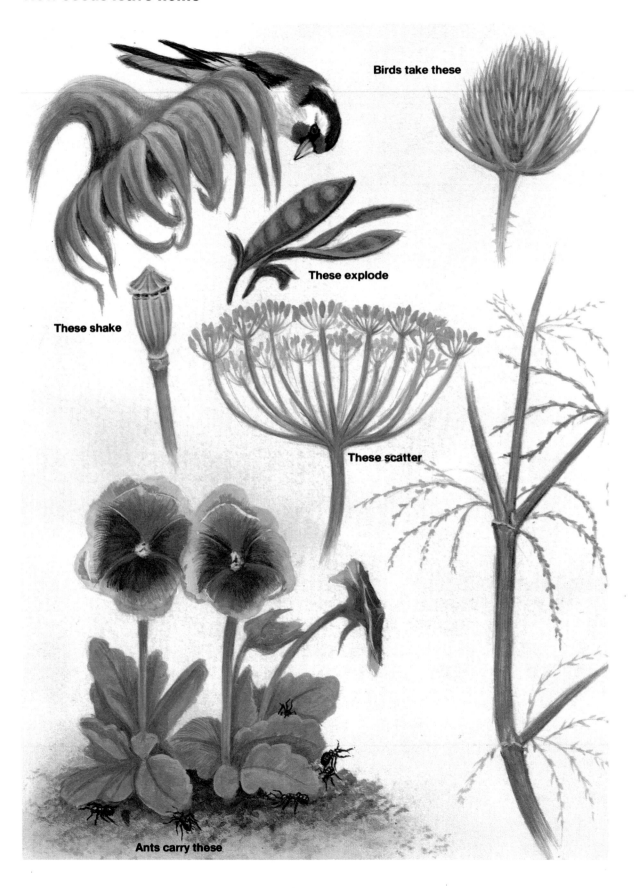

Birds take these

These explode

These shake

These scatter

Ants carry these

24

Action centre — seeds

When pollen from the anthers of one flower has arrived on the stigma of another flower of the same kind, the flower sets seeds. Bright colours are no longer needed to attract the insects and the flowers die away.

Flowers store seeds   Each dead flower has a swollen seed box called an ovary. Look for it in different places on the dead flowers.

Seed patterns   Carefully cut across the green seed boxes of different flowers and find the unripe seeds. They are arranged in special patterns for each plant family. Seed patterns make good designs for potato prints!

Leaving home   Seeds move away from their parent plant so they can have plenty of room to grow. Some blow away, some shake away. And there are floaters, twisters, and even some exploders!

Floaters and twisters   When you have explored your flower bed, find some dandelion and sycamore seeds. They are floaters and spinners, but can you see how they work? See if you can make some flying models!

Ant wages   Flowers in the pansy family use ants to spread their seeds. The ants take the seeds away and eat just part of them. Then the seeds grow where the ants left them!

Collecting seeds   If you want to collect some seeds to grow, wait until they are dry and brown. Collect them on a sunny day and put them in paper (not plastic) envelopes and keep them in a cool place. A warm room would kill them.

Paths and pavements

A sunny path or patio is a garden desert. There is very little soil where seeds can take root. Damp, soft-bodied animals like worms and slugs dry up and die if they are caught here in the sunshine.

Make a magnifier!   To discover the pavement desert, you need a magnifier. You can make your own if you have not got one in your **Nit kit**.

Use a wax crayon or birthday cake candle to draw a tiny circle inside a clear plastic lid or dish.

Put a droplet of water exactly inside the waxy circle, with your **Nit kit** eye dropper. Then use the droplet as a magnifying glass!

Now you can explore the secrets of the tiny things you find on paths.

Plants without flowers

Moss caps   Some mosses may look as if they have brown hairs. Use your magnifier to look more closely and you will see that they are little spore boxes, just like pixie caps.

Liverwort umbrellas   In spring, you might find a liverwort sprouting with tiny umbrellas! These are the male and female parts of the liverwort which help it to make spores.

Growing a dust trap   The wind blows dust into the cracks of the pavement desert. Sometimes there are seeds in the dust, but they cannot grow without water. Sprinkle some pavement dust into a flower pot. Water it, then put the pot inside a plastic bag. Wait for a week or so to see what treasures the wind has blown in!

PLANTED ON 3RD JUNE

The dry pavement

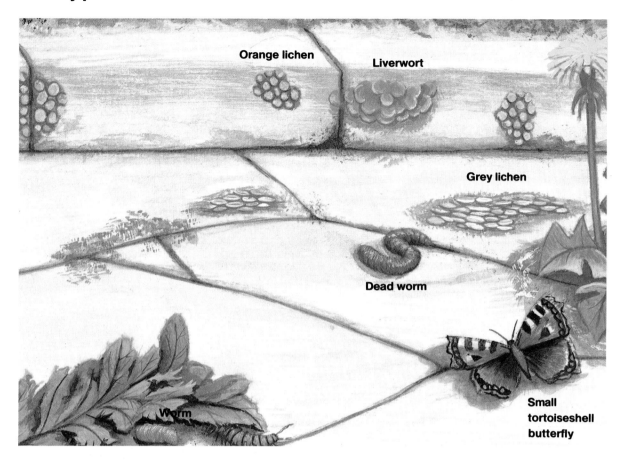

Orange lichen
Liverwort
Grey lichen
Dead worm
Worm
Small tortoiseshell butterfly

The survivors   Animals like beetles and ants have their skeletons outside. The hard, shiny surface stops them from drying up, so they can move safely in hot, dry places.

The visible ants' nest   Ants can even live under the pavement desert! Watch for them coming and going carrying food. Close to their nest, you will find fresh, disturbed dust with tiny holes in it. If you find the nest, ask if you can make an observation station. Then collect together a square of stiff, clear plastic and a piece of black bin liner of the same size. Have them all ready before you begin because ants are fast!

Take up the paving stone over the nest and put the plastic in its place.

Put the piece of bin liner over the clear plastic and weigh the corners down with stones.

The ants do not seem to notice that their roof has changed! When you want to see what they are doing, you can just look quickly under the bin liner layer.

The dark damp pavement

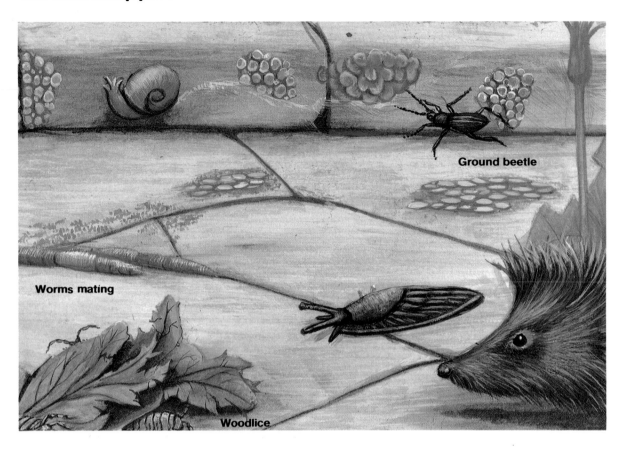

Ground beetle

Worms mating

Woodlice

The night shift At night after rain, the pavement bustles with life. It is cool and wet enough for the soft, slimy animals who come out, although danger is never very far behind! Beetles, centipedes, or even a hedgehog, will also be out hunting for a juicy slug or worm. Using your torch with a red cellophane cover, you can watch what happens.

Put a big worm on a piece of rough paper. It has bristles underneath to help it to crawl. Make a paper ear-trumpet, and listen to the bristles scratching the paper as the worm moves.

See how they run (or slide!)
Catch a slug or snail with your **Nit kit** plastic spoon. Put your catch inside a jam jar, leave it to settle and then look at it from underneath. You can see the muscles rippling as it glides over the glass. Can you find its eyes?

If you catch a centipede or millipede, put it on some dry sand. It will leave tiny footprints and a mark which shows that its body touches the ground as it runs.

Watch the creatures for just a few minutes, then let them go free in a damp, dark place.

Mating worms Worms may come up from two different holes in the pavement and begin to mate. There are no male and female worms! After they have mated, each will lay eggs inside a little lemon-shaped cocoon made by the worm's 'saddle'.

Saddle

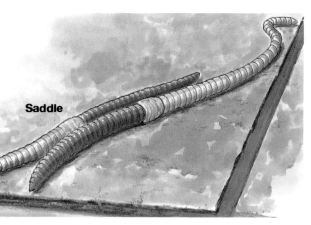

Making a choice chamber Test some woodlice to see if they do choose to live only in damp, dark places. You will need some thin card, some sticky tape, cotton wool, and a shallow box with a clear lid. The kind you buy full of Christmas cards is just right.

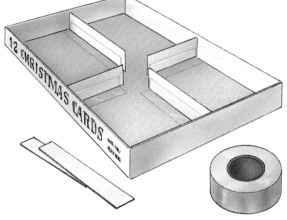

Glue some strips of card inside the box, to make four rooms, with a space in the middle.

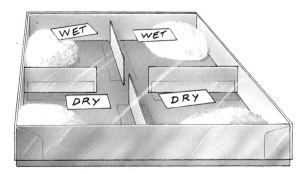

Put dry cotton wool in two of the little rooms, and wet cotton wool in the other two.

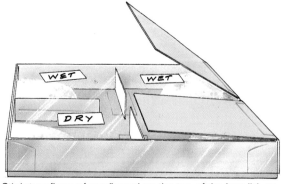

Stick two flaps of cardboard on the top of the box lid, so that they can be lifted up like trap doors.

And now for the woodlice! Use your **Nit kit** paintbrush to pick up several woodlice, and put them into the box. Put the lid on with the flaps down, and leave them for two hours.

The woodlice will have chosen the most comfortable spot to stay. Make a guess before you look to find them!

Logs

Making a log habitat

Not every garden has a log pile, although you can often find one in the country, or in a park. If you can make one in your own garden, extra wildlife will soon drop in—and stay! You may find a park keeper or farmer who has two or three logs to spare if you ask. You do not need very many.

Reading a log   Read your log's life story before you use it!

Count the rings   Look at the cut side of the log and you will find that it shows light and dark coloured rings. The tree grows one ring of each colour every year. So if you count just the dark ones, you will find out how old the tree was when it was cut down.

Where's the sunny side?   If the tree was growing at the edge of a wood, one side would get more sunshine than the other. Trees use sunlight to help them to make food, so the tree rings will be fatter on the sunny side.

After a dry summer   Sometimes, the weather is too dry for the tree to grow very much. When this happens, you will find two of the dark rings very close together.

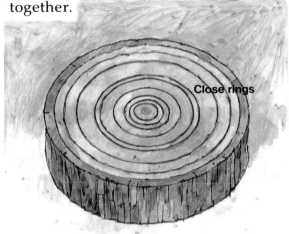

Close rings

Branching out   See if you can find what happens to a log when a branch starts to grow from deep inside the trunk.

Setting up the habitat

The perfect place for a log habitat is in a cool, shady place under bushes or trees. Sprinkle a thick layer of garden compost or dead leaves on the ground, and put the logs on top of it. Arrange them so that they look attractive, and make good hiding places by leaving small gaps between them. Sprinkle some twigs and dead leaves over the gaps. If a hedgehog or toad could find a warm corner here for hibernation, your log habitat is a good one.

New log habitat

Annual rings

Compost

Time lapse snaps When you have set your logs into place, everything will look rather new and bare. There will be no plants and very few creatures to see. But you will be very surprised to find how quickly wildlife moves in. Make yourself a recording station by putting down two markers, one for each foot.

JAN 1   FEB 1   MARCH 1
APR 1   MAY 1   JUNE 1
JULY 1

On a special day of every month, take a photograph of the log habitat with your toes against the markers, so you always record from exactly the same spot. Mount the pictures on a sheet, and watch the habitat change.

LEFT
RIGHT

Wasp watching One of the first visitors early in spring might be a queen wasp, rasping at the wood to make paper to build her nest. You will be able to hear her jaws scraping away at the wood. If you have them, use binoculars to watch her at work

Old log habitat

- Sulphur tuft fungus
- Bracket fungus
- Toad
- Spider cocoon
- Woodlice
- Centipede
- Garlic snail

One year later . . . the habitat will look quite different, full of fungi, small creatures and wild flowers. The first plants there will be the kinds that can grow and flower all in the same year. They are called annuals.

Look for these

Chickweed

Chickweed flowers are smaller than your little fingernail. Use your magnifying glass and you will find how pretty they really are.

Shepherd's purse

Once the flower has gone, open up some of the tiny heart-shaped seed cases. They come easily into two halves. The seeds are like money in the shepherd's purse!

Pineapple weed

There are several flowers in this family, but you will know if yours is pineapple weed if you pinch one of the flower heads and sniff!

Underwood city

Animals without backbones are called *invertebrates*. You will find hundreds of them crowding into the cool darkness under logs.

There are often many shapes and sizes in each family, so look for different kinds of slugs, woodlice, centipedes, millipedes, beetles, snails, and spiders. To start you off, here are some portraits of members of the slug family.

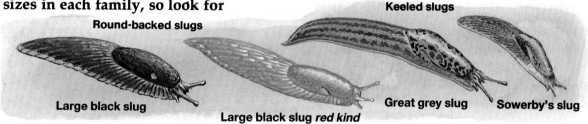

Round-backed slugs

Large black slug

Large black slug *red kind*

Keeled slugs

Great grey slug **Sowerby's slug**

Who comes home? Collect and count all the big garden snails from under the logs. Dot the **underneath** of their shells with coloured nail varnish. If you colour their backs, they will lose their camouflage! At night they will glide out to hunt for food. Then you can check how many marked ones come back home in the morning!

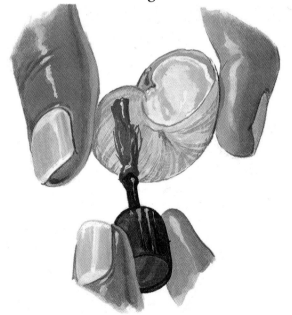

Sorting them out Use your magnifying glass to find out which invertebrates are predators, and which are prey. The predators have fierce, biting jaws!

Signposts Look for tracks and signs. You will find pearly eggs of slugs and snails like moist beads, and the silky cocoons of spider eggs. Nibble marks will be left on fungi by creatures which fed on them during the night. You might also find empty nuts and seed cases with small holes in them, chewed by a hungry mouse or vole.

The vertebrates Animals which have backbones, like mice and voles, are called vertebrates. Other vertebrates which use the logs to hibernate or to rest during the day will be frogs, toads, and newts. So turn your logs carefully! **Always put the logs back exactly as they were, so the habitat will not be spoilt.**

Ponds

Watch and wait

If you stay very still and quiet next to the pond, the creatures will not be disturbed and you can watch what they do. Insects will climb down plant stems to drink, and flies will parade round the water-lily leaves. The great pond snail will glide across the water, upside-down, and you can watch its breathing hole open to take in the air.

The water skiers!   Pond skaters will be moving swiftly over the water surface. But how do they stay up? Try some pond skater experiments.

Spreading the load
See if you can borrow two bathroom scales. Weigh yourself, and then stand with one foot on each. What happens to your weight? The pond skater uses four of its six legs to share its weight out over the water's surface.

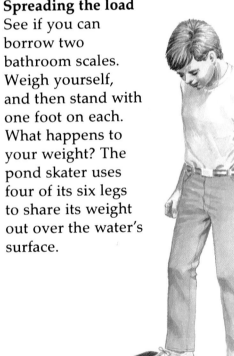

Waxy feet   Pond skaters have waxy feet to stop them from getting wet. To prove that it works, use wax crayons to draw a pond skater picture. Then gently go all over your picture with a light coloured paint or ink. Did your pond skater picture soak up the paint?

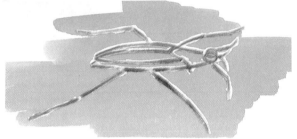

Skater senses   If a small creature falls in, the skater can feel its struggles and rushes across to catch it. Try tickling the surface of the water with a blade of grass. Does the skater come to investigate?

Pond partners   If your pond is big enough to have a dragonfly visitor, watch to see where it settles. Some kinds of dragonfly have a special perch to hunt from. If you sit absolutely still next to that spot without letting your shadow fall on it, the dragonfly may come and sit next to you. Do not breathe—just watch!

Above the pond

Yellow iris

Bogbean

Pond skater

Great pond snail

Under the water

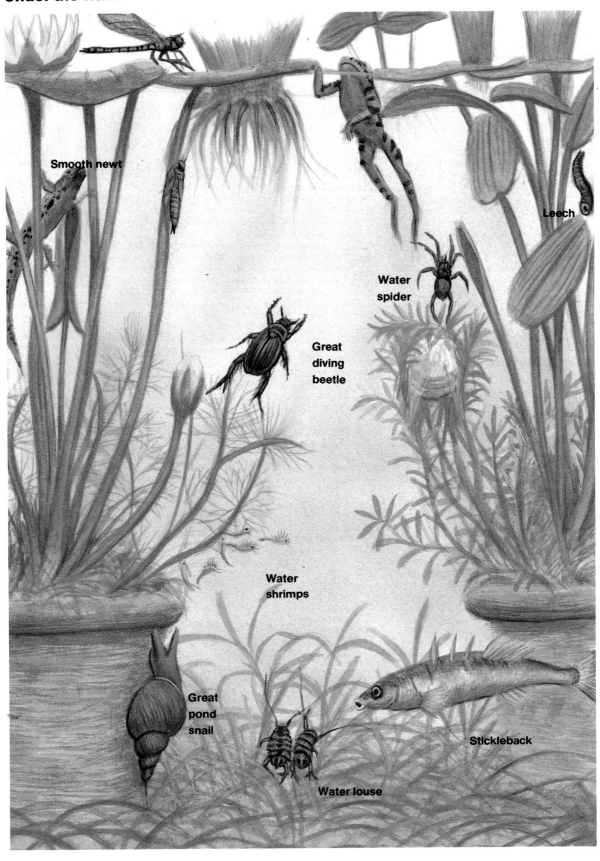

Smooth newt

Leech

Water spider

Great diving beetle

Water shrimps

Great pond snail

Water louse

Stickleback

Pond dipping

You will need a net to go pond dipping. You can make one by sewing old net curtains onto a wire frame made from a coat hanger. Easier still, you can use a plastic vegetable strainer and a garden cane.

Most vegetable strainers have gaps in their handles. Just push the garden cane through and over the gaps. Keep pushing until the stick rests against the mesh. If your strainer does not have a gap in its handle, you will have to tie the stick to it very tightly.

Mini nets
An old tea strainer makes an excellent mini net. You will see plenty of things happening because you will have to get really close to the water!

Sorting the catch
Turn your net upside-down into a white ice cream container with some pond water in it. The creatures will show up clearly against the white background. Watch the way they move.

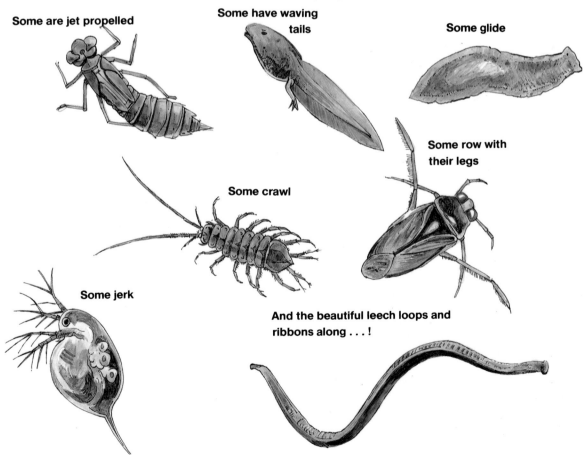

Some are jet propelled

Some have waving tails

Some glide

Some row with their legs

Some crawl

Some jerk

And the beautiful leech loops and ribbons along . . . !

A mini pond

If there is no pond close to home where you can go dipping, you can make your own mini pond. During the summer, dig a hole and line it with a big strong plastic bag. Tuck the edges down to stop it blowing about, and fill it with water. Easier still, leave a washing up bowl of water outside in the garden or on your balcony. Do not put your mini pond right under a tree, it needs to get some sunshine.

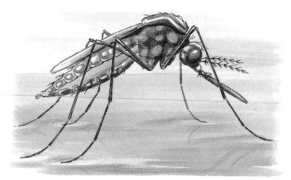

Then at last, the adult mosquito struggles out of the pupal skin, and dries out on the pond surface ready to fly away.

Mosquito life cycle

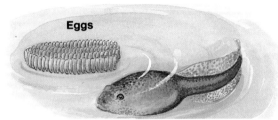

When your mini pond has been outside for about a week, you will probably see a tiny raft floating on top of the water. It is made out of lots of tiny upright eggs laid there by a mosquito.

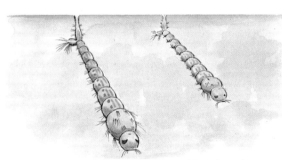

The mosquito larvae soon hatch out. They breathe through a tube at their tail ends and will swim jerkily down to the bottom if your shadow falls on the mini pond.

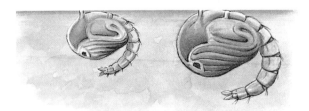

When the larva has changed into a pupa, there is an air space inside its big head. That means it must float head upwards, breathing through two tiny trumpets at the back.

Life cycle wheel

Take two circles of thin card, and make a life cycle wheel like this:

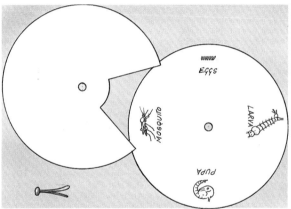

Draw the mosquito life cycle round one of the circles.

Cut a wedge out of the second card.

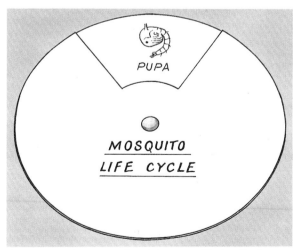

Put the cut piece over the pictures, and fasten the two circles together with a 'butterfly' paper clip.

Turn the wheel to show how the mosquitoes grow!

The indoor mini pond

Even if you have not got a garden at all, do not despair, there are investigations for you too! All you need are some good friends, and a big plastic sweet bottle (they give these away free from most sweet shops).

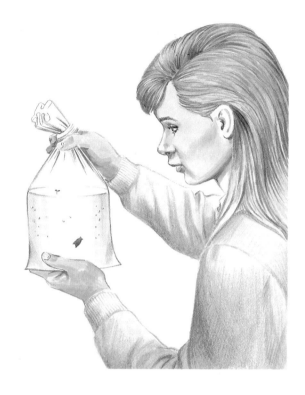

Fill your sweet bottle nearly up to the neck with water and leave it on a sunny window ledge for a few days. Soon you will notice that the water and the sides of the bottle have gone green.

From your good friends (or the pet shop!) you need:
A great pond snail
Some daphnia
And one—just one—tiny floating duckweed plant

The lightning licker!   The green in the sweet jar is caused by microscopic green plants. The pond snail loves them! Put it into the jar, and watch it climb up the side. If you look carefully, you will see its tongue poking in and out as it eats its way along. Just like a lawnmower, it leaves a clear path behind it!

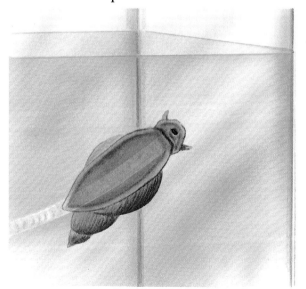

Clean water too?
The daphnia eat the little green plants that are floating in the water. How long will it take them to clean the water? Try looking at them with your magnifying glass too. You can see eggs inside their special pouch and watch their hearts beating!

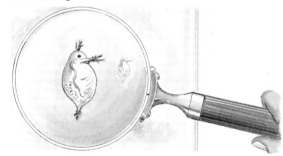

The double act
Duck weed just keeps on doubling! Float one plant on the water. Every day, count how many leaves there are. Perhaps you could work out how many there would be after a year.

Trees

Summer trees

Some kinds of trees have grown in Britain for thousands of years, but some have been brought to this country by keen gardeners because of their beauty. Which group of trees do you think will be best for wildlife?

The Nit squad hoover! To find out, you will need a 'pooter'. Collect together a small jar, some old tights, a small rubber band, and about 50 cm of plastic tubing from an aquarium shop.

You may need some help to make two holes in the lid of the jar, for the tubing. Then you put the pooter together like this:

Who lives up there? Hook the handle of an umbrella over a branch and give it a firm shake. Ask permission if you are working outside your own garden, and do not damage the tree! The tree creatures will fall safely into your umbrella.

Poot them up! You will need to act quickly to stop your catch from escaping! You can lift the larger creatures with a soft paintbrush, but that might damage the smaller ones. Point the long end of the pooter at each one, and suck sharply on the short end. The tights material is to save you from a nasty experience!

The best tree house Count your catch and choose one or two to make huge drawings for your **Nit squad** office. Then try some more trees to find which kind is home to the most creatures.

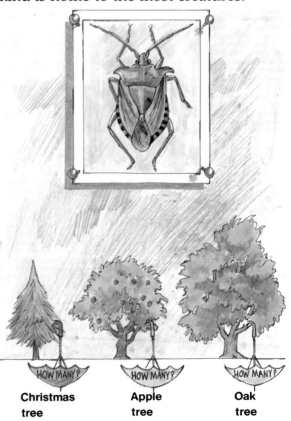

Christmas tree   Apple tree   Oak tree

The tree factory

First, free your tree creatures back into the branches. Then, think about the tree itself. Why is it that trees and plants are so important to us?

Green plants and trees are the only living things which can make food by catching and using warmth and light from the sun.

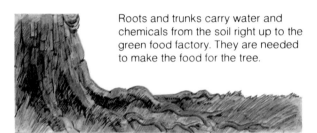

Roots and trunks carry water and chemicals from the soil right up to the green food factory. They are needed to make the food for the tree.

Dead leaves under the tree are slowly turned back into soil, so that their chemicals can be used again. Dig down and try to find little pieces of leaves in the soil. Fungi and small creatures have helped to break them up.

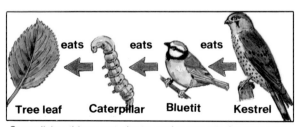

Tree leaf   eats   Caterpillar   eats   Bluetit   eats   Kestrel

Some living things eat plants, and some eat the creatures which eat plants. In this food chain, can you see why the kestrel would die if there were no plants? Make up some more food chains and find out if this is always true.

Trees in summer

Silver birch

Apple

Holly

Spruce

Trees in winter

Trees which drop their leaves late in the autumn are called *deciduous* trees. Evergreen trees lose their leaves too, but just a few at a time all the year round. So they really are ever green!

Elastic band

Why lose leaves? Find an evergreen and a deciduous tree, and fasten a plastic sandwich bag over a twig of each tree. Leave it for a whole day. What do you notice when you come back?

Leaves lose water All trees lose some water through tiny holes in their leaves, but the waxy, shiny coat on evergreen leaves like holly and bay, keeps at least some of the water in. Much more water escapes from deciduous leaves.

In winter there is little sunshine to help the trees make food. The soil is sometimes frozen hard. The roots cannot suck up water. So deciduous trees drop their leaves. Very little precious water will be lost. The beautiful autumn colours of the dead leaves are made by waste materials which the tree does not need. Everything goes back to the soil to be used again.

Silver birch

Apple

Spruce

Holly

Leaf skeleton Christmas cards   Look among the leaf litter under the trees. Sometimes parts of a leaf rot away leaving just a beautiful skeleton. You can paint the skeleton silver, and use it to make a Christmas card.

How old is this tree?   Trees which make their seeds in cones are called *coniferous* trees. Each year, new branches grow from the top. It is easy to count the rings of branches, and tell the tree's age.

Twigs tell the time!   At the end of a deciduous twig you will find a bud. Inside it are new leaves, ready for spring. Each year, when the new leaves burst from their bud, a scar is left on the twig. If you count the bud scars you can discover how many years it has taken the twig to grow!

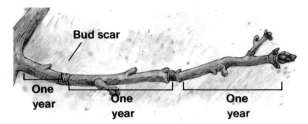

Bud scar

One year   One year   One year

A twig plaster cast

You can recognise a tree even without its leaves if you learn its special bud shape and the patterns the buds make as they grow from the twig.

Make a plaster cast collection of different winter twigs to help you remember.

You will need some plasticine, a margarine tub, some water, a winter twig, and some plaster of Paris. You can buy plaster of Paris from a chemist's shop.

Flatten the plasticine and press the winter twig into it. Take it out and it will leave its shape stamped into the plasticine.

Cut the bottom from the margarine tub and press it down round the twig shape, like a picture frame.

Put some plaster in an old jug and mix it with enough water to make it look like thin cream. Quickly pour the mixture into the margarine tub frame and leave it to set hard. Then peel the plasticine off and find your winter twig model!

MARGARINE

The Nit squad action centre

Natural Investigators always seem to make huge collections of things! Sometimes they get stuffed into cupboards and forgotten, but it is far better to turn them into your own mini museum. Here are some ideas to help you.

Quick shelves   You can use bricks and thick cardboard to make shelves for special things. Make them different heights so you can see them clearly.

Small treasures   Tiny things are best kept in small boxes where they will not get squashed. Glue them to the bottom if they are very fragile.

Leaves and flowers   Pressed and dried leaves and flowers can be kept in a book. Cover them with see-through book film to keep them safe.

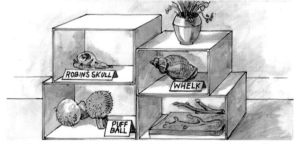

Another way is to fasten cardboard boxes together, like a bookcase.

Feathers   Stick feathers into corks. Then you can handle them, and they will not get spoiled.

A zig zag book   If you want to record something that changed as the days went by, a zig zag book is ideal!

Remember   Check that nobody minds before you make any big changes to your room!

44

The Nit squad code

Nit squad people want to find out about living things, so they have to collect things, make investigations and keep records. However, the best naturalists would never do anything to spoil any habitat, or to spoil other people's enjoyment. There have to be just a few rules!

About living creatures

Remember that living creatures have feelings too. Make a mini habitat for them in your collecting jars, but put them back in their own habitat as soon as you have finished looking at them.

Keep well away from nesting birds

You must never collect amphibians, reptiles or mammals from the wild. It is cruel to do so, and very often against the law.

Leave every habitat just as you found it! It is easy to forget to put a rolled log back!

About plants

It is against the law to dig up plants outside your own garden without permission from the person whose land it is.

By all means take one leaf from a plant for your collection, but leave the flowers for other people to enjoy. You can collect just a few seeds from common flowers to grow in your own garden.

Do not damage trees or plants. Even fungi should be left for other people's excitement!

About other people

Never make changes in your house or garden without checking first.

Never leave litter to spoil other people's enjoyment.

Always tell the people at home or at school if you are off on an investigation. They need to know where you are.

It all sounds very glum, but it is a serious business. A good naturalist always thinks twice before acting once!

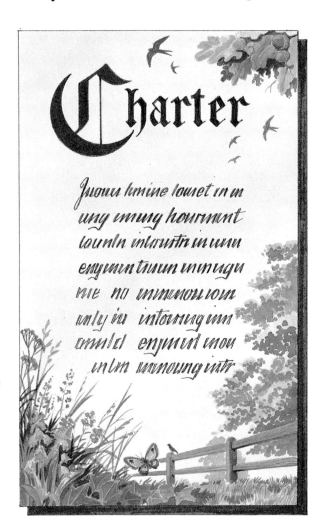

Useful words

Anther
The male part of a flower, from which the pollen comes.

Cocoon
A parcel spun by insects and spiders from their silk. It is used to keep eggs or pupae safe.

Daphnia
Little creatures living in water. They are often called water fleas.

Deciduous tree
One which loses its leaves in winter.

Frond
The feathery leaf of a fern.

Habitat
A place that is just right for the animals and plants which live in it.

Invertebrate
A creature which has no backbone.

Larva
A young creature, such as a caterpillar, which is very much different from its parents.

Lichen
A plant which is really a sort of team. The two partners are a fungus, and a tiny green plant, working together to make food.

Moulting
Furry animals and birds moult when they lose their fur or feathers, ready to grow a new coat.

Nectar
Sweet sticky juice made by flowers to attract insects to them.

Ovary
The seed box of a flower.

Pollen
The special dust which comes from the anthers of a flower. Without it flowers cannot make seeds.

Preening
Birds are said to be preening when they clean and comb their feathers.

Pupa
The resting stage of a larva, during which it changes its shape into an adult.

Sorus
The mark under a fern's leaf where its spores come from. The plural is 'sori'.

Stigma
The female part of the flower. The pollen sticks to it so that it can make seeds.

Vertebrate
A creature which has a backbone.

Useful addresses
If you are a Natural Investigator working alone at home, sometimes it is more fun to be part of a team! If you are already part of a **Nit squad**, it would be great to share your investigations with other people. You might like to join one of these clubs:

RSPCA,
Junior membership
Causeway
Horsham
West Sussex
RH12 1 HG

Young Ornithologists' Club,
The Lodge
Sandy
Bedfordshire
SG19 2DL

'WATCH'
The Royal Society for Nature Conservation,
22 The Green
Nettleham
Lincoln
LN2 2NR

The Young Peoples' Trust for Endangered Species
95 Woodbridge Road
Guildford
Surrey
GU1 4BB

Asda Nature Watch
East Street
Petworth
Sussex
GU28 0AB

Software
Also available from BBC Enterprises:
Make a wildlife garden (ISBN 0 563 22894 6)
Bird spy (ISBN 0 563 22857 1)
Software for BBC micros models B, B+, Master 128 and Master Compact

Contact BBC School Publications,
PO Box 234, Weatherby,
West Yorkshire, LS23 7EU

Published by BBC Educational Publishing,
a division of BBC Enterprises Limited,
Woodlands, 80 Wood Lane, London W12 0TT
First published 1989
Reprinted 1992

Paperback ISBN: 0 563 34499 7
Hardback ISBN: 0 563 34498 9

Printed in Great Britain by BPCC Paulton Books Limited,
Typeset by Ace Filmsetting, England
Origination by Dot Gradations, England